Turning Back the Pages
Ravenshead

Introduction

Ravenshead is situated about four miles south of Mansfield and ten miles north of Nottingham. The village grew out of a number of distinct residential areas in the 20th century, including Fishpool, Larch Farm, Abbey Gates and Kighill, which formed parts of the parish of Blidworth and the Liberty of Newstead. The names Ravenshead and Kighill for parts of the area can be traced back to at least the 12th century. Much of the area was originally covered by large tracts of sandy heath, consisting of gorse and heather, interspersed with deciduous woodland of oak, beech, silver birch and sweet chestnut. With the enclosure of land and improvements in agriculture in the late 18th and early 19th centuries, new farms were built and the hamlet of Fishpool was established with the building of sixteen cottages on Fishpool Hill (now Robin Hood Terrace) about 1833.

Most of the development in the area did not take place until after the First World War. The first houses to be built in the Abbey Gates and Larch Farm areas were on Nottingham Road, Main Road, Sheepwalk Lane, Vernon Avenue and Longdale Lane, in the 1920s and 1930s. Large-scale building did not commence until about 1952, with the greatest increase in housing occurring in the 1960s and 1970s, when the estates on the north side of Longdale Lane were developed. A new ecclesiastical parish was formed in 1971 and a civil parish in 1987. In 1966, when the area became known officially as Ravenshead, there were about 3,000 inhabitants. By 2001 the population had increased to 5,636.

Philip E. Jones

Front cover: St. Peter's Church, c.1996. The silver birch trees in front of the church have since been removed.

© Philip E. Jones 2009

ISBN 978-0-902751-64-4

On 22nd March 1966 the largest find of medieval gold coins in Britain was made by workmen clearing the land for housing, where Cambourne Gardens now stands. The Fishpool Gold Hoard consisted of 1,237 coins dating mainly from the reigns of Edward III and Edward IV, plus nine items of jewellery. It may have originally formed part of the Lancastrian royal treasury entrusted to someone fleeing south after the Battle of Hexham in May 1464 (© *Trustees of the British Museum*).

The Hutt, Nottingham Road, c.1905. The signboard proudly advertises 'The Hutt Temperance Hotel. Parties catered for. British wines. Minerals. Teas. Hot water. Cigars. M. Bailey, proprietor.'

Extensive alterations and additions were carried out to The Hutt in the mid-1930s, when this Italianate marble fireplace, dated c.1820, was installed in the dining room. It was reputed to have come from Ilam Hall in Staffordshire, but was removed during refurbishment in 2000.

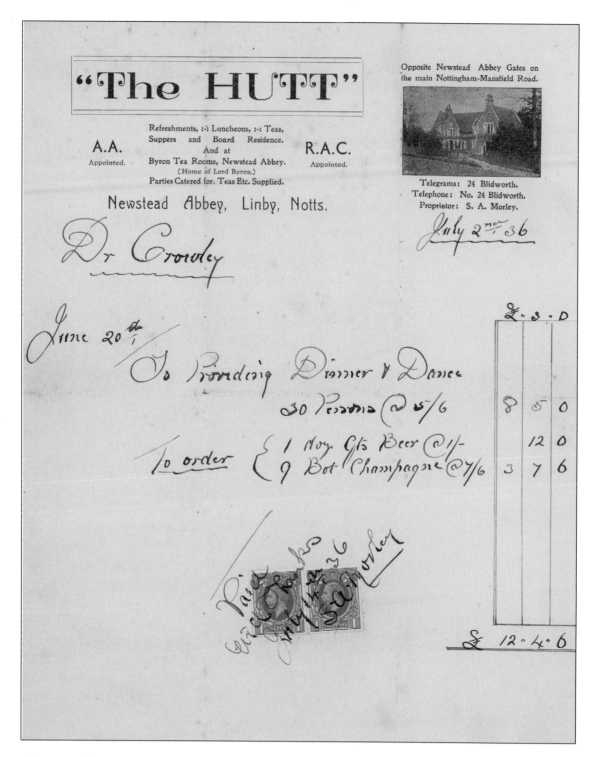

"The HUTT"

A.A. Appointed.

Refreshments, :-: Luncheons, :-: Teas, Suppers and Board Residence.
And at
Byron Tea Rooms, Newstead Abbey.
(Home of Lord Byron.)
Parties Catered for. Teas Etc. Supplied.

R.A.C. Appointed.

Opposite Newstead Abbey Gates on the main Nottingham-Mansfield Road.

Telegrams: 24 Blidworth.
Telephone: No. 24 Blidworth.
Proprietor: S. A. Morley.

Newstead Abbey, Linby, Notts.

July 2nd 36

Dr Crowley

	£	s	D
June 20th / To Providing Dinner & Dance 30 Persons @ 5/6	8	5	0
To order { 1 doz Gts Beer @1/-		12	0
{ 9 Bot Champagne @7/6	3	7	6
£	12	4	6

Paid Crowley 20/7/36
with thanks S A Morley

The Hotel was a popular venue for social events in the 1930s. This bill from 1936 shows a dinner dance for thirty people costing £8 5s 0d (excluding drinks), equivalent to just over £300 today. Even the champagne seems reasonable at 7s 6d per bottle (about £14 today).

"The Hutt" Hotel

DIRECTORS:
S. A. MORLEY.   J. WILLIAMSON.
A. MORLEY.   J. WILLIAMSON.

Newstead Abbey, Linby, Notts.

Fully Licensed : Residential

Weddings.
Private Parties Catered for.

TELEPHONE } BLIDWORTH
TELEGRAMS } 224

Wedding reception at The Hutt, 9th October 1936. The bride was Amy Gee, daughter of a well-known Sutton wallpaper and paint merchant. The groom was Clarence Bacon, senior lecturer in building construction at the County Technical College, Mansfield. The author's father, Hugh Jones, was one of the groomsmen and is standing at the far right of the photograph, gloves in hand.

Little John public house, c.1900. Rowland Ward, a Blidworth draper, built the Little John about 1837. He also built the row of cottages on Fishpool Hill (now Robin Hood Terrace). The pub was acquired by the Mansfield Brewery Company in 1903.

V.E. Day, 1945. A group of local schoolchildren and mothers gathered outside the Little John to celebrate Victory in Europe Day on 8 May 1945, at the end of the Second World War.

Slaney Stone, Chapel Lane. One of the regulars at the Little John public house in the 1890s was John Slaney, a local farmer, who lived at Longdale Farm. On the night of 24th January 1893 he was returning home drunk on his horse and cart. It would appear that he had stood up to relieve himself and had fallen headfirst onto the road. He was found dead by his wife, Hannah, who had gone to look for him. He was buried in Blidworth churchyard and this memorial stone was placed on Chapel Lane to mark the spot where he was found.

Fishpool Farm, Main Road, in 1993. The name of the old hamlet of Fishpool is preserved in this farm's name. The style and layout of the buildings suggest it was built in the late 18th century. The derelict buildings shown here were demolished in 2005 and a new dwelling constructed.

Larch Farm, Mansfield Road, in the 1950s. The farm was built about 1831-32 and took its name from nearby larch plantations. In the 1950s its pedigree herd of Essex saddle back pigs was well known in the area.

William Hollins (1862-1918) of Berry Hill Hall, Mansfield. He was a director of William Hollins & Company Ltd., textile manufacturers, of Pleasley Vale, and owned Larch Farm from 1897 until his death in 1918. He never lived there, but let the farm out to various tenants.

Larch Farm in 1993. The farm and outbuildings stood empty for a number of years before being extensively renovated and converted into a public house, which opened in 1996.

Longdale Farm, 1933. The farm dates from the mid-19th century. This postcard shows the farmhouse in the summer of 1933, after the Youth Hostels Association had converted it into a hikers' hostel with accommodation for twenty-four people.

A camp site ready equipped for twenty people was established by the Youth Hostels Association on land adjacent to the farmhouse. Both the hostel and the camp site appear to have been short-lived.

George and Susan Walker were tenant farmers at Longdale Farm in the 1930s.

Aerial view of Longdale Farm in 1972, before the outbuildings were converted into a craft centre.

In 1972 Ravenshead sculptor Gordon Brown, seen here, acquired a collection of ramshackle tin-roofed buildings, which had been the chicken sheds belonging to Longdale Farm and converted them into the now internationally-renowned Longdale Craft Centre. The site today offers a gallery, restaurant, museum, and antiques and collectables centre.

Sunrise Poultry Farm, Chapel Lane, in the 1950s. This farm was on the west side of Chapel Lane (seen in the foreground), just north of the present junction with Church Drive. Much of the surrounding land was sold in 1960 to the Nottingham building firm, Rostance, for housing.

Hutt Farm, Longdale Lane, in the 1950s. The Hutt Inn originally formed part of the Newstead Abbey estate and was usually let together with a farm of eighty acres – the Hutt Farm. It ceased to be a working farm in the 1960s and the original farmhouse was converted into flats now known as Hutt Farm Court.

A kitchen garden, with fruit trees and a greenhouse, belonging to the Hutt Farm can just be made out in this photograph taken in January 1963. The site is now occupied by The Hutt car park.

The A60 Nottingham Road was much quieter when this photograph was taken in January 1963. Note the Longdale Lane junction before the road layout was altered and the old signpost and telephone kiosk long since gone.

The public footpath from Nottingham Road to Sheepwalk Lane, through Sheepwalk Plantation, autumn 1982. The path is now tarmacked and the silver birches were felled when the houses on Pilgrim Close were built.

St. Peter's Church Hall, Sheepwalk Lane.

An ex-army hut (sectional building) was purchased from the Ministry of Works in November 1946 and erected with the help of founder members of the church. It served the dual purposes of worship and social life until the new St. Peter's Church was built in 1971.

The Bishop of Southwell, Dr. F.R. Barry, and church choir, at the dedication of St. Peter's, 29th June 1948.

The Gilbert & Sullivan Society was among the first of many church organisations. In this 1957 production of the Mikado, the part of Katisha was played by Mary Williamson and that of Ko-Ko by Peter Garratt. Mary Williamson founded the G.& S. Society and was also a founder member of St. Peter's Church and its choirmaster and organist for many years.

The new St. Peter's Church – building in progress, June 1971. Here we see the shape of the roofline behind the altar. The church is of an unconventional style, being elliptical in shape and featuring a catenary timber shell roof, designed to be in keeping with the then modern housing development taking place in the area.

Right Reverend Denis Wakeling, Bishop of Southwell, officiated at the dedication service of the new church on 22nd April 1972, assisted by the Archdeacon of Newark, Venerable Brian Woodhams, and the vicar of St. Peter's, Reverend Barrie Hodges.

Aerial view of
Ravenshead, 1972

Free Methodist Chapel, Chapel Lane, April 1955. Built in 1864, the chapel was reputedly the smallest in Nottinghamshire, measuring only twenty-seven feet by twenty-five feet. It stood near the junction with Bretton Road and gave the name to Chapel Lane, which had previously been known as Papplewick Road *(Nottingham City Council, photographed by G. Denison).*

Chapel interior. Members of the Hayes and Hall families, who lived on Robin Hood Terrace, and who were closely associated with the chapel before the Second World War.

The chapel was demolished in 1960 by a Mansfield joiner, Harry Maltby, who built a bungalow on the site. The chapel's founder, William Clay, had been buried under the aisle when he died in 1879. Prior to the chapel's demolition, his body was exhumed and re-interred in Blidworth churchyard.

Blidworth Dale House, 1961. In 1818 Samuel Parsons, a Nottingham solicitor, bought the 500-acre Blidworth Dale estate. He built a small farmhouse and farm buildings, and shortly afterwards he added this red brick mansion. The estate was owned by William Frederick Webb of Newstead Abbey in the 1890s. In 1961 the estate was sold by Mrs. Jessie Spencer to Captain Richard Abel-Smith(1933-2004), who was the great-great-grandson of Queen Victoria. *Nottinghamshire Archives DD 124/1*

Entrance Hall

Lounge showing fireplace and bay window.

Ravenshead Library and Health Centre, 1972. A new library combined with health centre was opened in January 1972. It was designed by Nottinghamshire County Council's Architects Department and built using the CLASP system of prefabricated building. The library had previously been accommodated in the village hall.
(Photographs courtesy of Nottinghamshire County Council Communities Department)

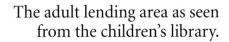
The adult lending area as seen from the children's library.

View of the children's library upstairs above the health centre.

View from the issue desk of the main health centre entrance
and the children's library upstairs.

Princess Alice, Countess of Athlone, and grandmother of Richard Abel-Smith of Blidworth Dale, laying the foundation stone of the Abbey Gates Village Hall, 29th May 1968.

Invited guests and residents of Ravenshead watch the laying of the foundation stone for the Village Hall, 29th May 1968. The houses in the background are on Vernon Crescent.

7509. NEWSTEAD HOSPITAL. FISHPOOL. NOTTS.

Newstead Hospital, Kirkby Road, August 1946. Opened in 1942 by the City of Nottingham as a sanatorium for the treatment of pulmonary tuberculosis, it became a hospital for the elderly and infirm in 1970. The hospital closed in 1992 and was demolished to make way for housing, most of the houses on High Leys Drive being completed by 1997 *(© English Heritage, NMR, Aerofilms Collection).*

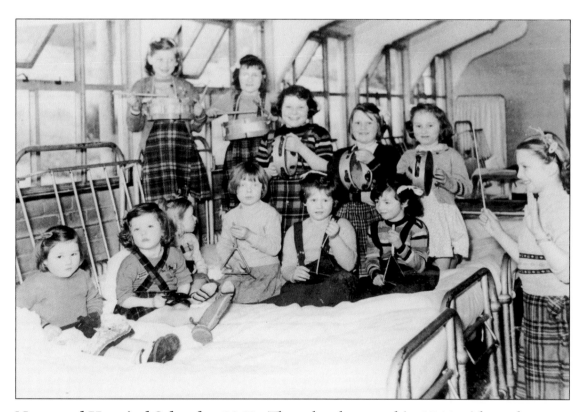

Newstead Hospital School, c.1960. The school opened in 1944 with twelve small children, suffering from tuberculosis, on the roll. Over 900 children passed through the school before it closed in 1964. The children pictured here appear to have formed their own impromptu band.
Nottinghamshire Archives SBX 324/1

Milton Court shopping precinct under construction, December 1962. Looking west towards Milton Drive and Sheepwalk Lane.

Shopping precinct, 1969. The precinct is complete apart from the supermarket and health centre/library (yet to be built). Note how close people could park to the shops at this time.

The first supermarket (Mace) in Ravenshead was opened by Wilbourn's of Kirkby on 18th February 1971. The firm had previously been in business in the precinct for six years with a self-service shop on a much smaller scale. This photograph, taken soon after the store opened, shows some of the original staff encouraging people to come in and buy British produce.

Post Office, Main Road. Ravenshead originally had two post offices. The Fishpool Post Office and Newsagents, shown here, opened on Main Road about 1941. It closed in October 2000 on the retirement of the last sub postmaster and reverted to a private house.

"In 1930 we wanted to move from Hucknall and just above the Abbey Gates was a big board. It said: 'Land ½d. a yard'. My brother and myself had come out and seen it. We counted our savings up and said to my mother, 'we're going to buy some land'. This is what made her decide to come out here."

(Vera Cox, née Swinton, whose family gave the name to Swinton Rise).

"Green Gables", Longdale Lane. A timber-framed bungalow, typical of many huts built in the area just before the Second World War and originally used as weekend retreats. This one, which stood at the junction of Gorse Hill and Longdale Lane, was demolished and replaced by a modern brick bungalow in 1992.

Longdale Avenue, 1958. View looking up Longdale Avenue, from the junction with Longdale Lane. The sewer pipes are ready to be laid and the pavements have yet to be made up.

Regina Crescent, 1960. The author's family home for over fifty years. The half-acre plot, originally agricultural land, was purchased in 1957 for £600 and the bungalow was built in 1958 at a cost of £2,700. Note the unadopted road and the houses in the distance on Longdale Lane, not visible from this point today.

The sandstone quarries on Longdale Lane were originally opened in 1919 to supply building sand for Nottingham and Hucknall. When the quarries closed in November 1969 it is estimated that 1½ million tons of sand had been extracted. The houses on Quarry Road, Quarry Close and Sandfield Avenue now occupy this site.

Before the large housing estates were developed in the 1960s and 1970s, many people chose to build privately. Local contractors, such as F. Wright, would obviously have been in great demand at this time.

Longdale Avenue in the early 1960s, near the junction with Longdale Lane. In the distance are the back gardens of properties on Regina Crescent, abutting the Cornwater fields, with Kighill Wood on the horizon. The bungalow in the centre, on Longdale Lane, was later demolished and replaced by a modern house.

Church Drive, 1962, showing the limit of housing development at that time.
The path leading up the hillside is now the public footpath from Church Drive,
joining Milton Crescent beside the small wood (the large trees on the horizon)
at the end of Woodland Rise.

The end of Church Drive in 1962, looking north from the bottom of the
footpath in the previous photograph. The scrubby wasteland, covered in gorse,
in the distance would later become Southview Gardens and Swinton Rise.

View looking up Church Drive towards Sheepwalk Lane, 1962, showing the sandy nature of the terrain before the road was adopted. The author remembers it was very hazardous to cycle along as a small boy!

House foundations, Church Drive, in 1970. Bourne Drive and Cheriton Drive are just visible in the background. There were still substantial areas of gorse on Church Drive at this time, ideal habitat for linnets and rabbits!

Bourne Drive and Waltham Road, 1968. Newly-built houses. The mechanical digger is excavating a trench for the main sewers.

Bourne Drive, 1968. View looking down Bourne Drive to what is now a cul-de-sac. Beyond, in the distance, are Church Drive and the bottom end of Mavis Avenue, awaiting development.

Aerial view of the west side of Gorse Hill, formerly called Linnet Hill, in the 1980s. On the left can be seen part of McCarthy's sand quarry, which was later filled in and developed for housing, now The Heyes and Misterton Crescent.

Cornwater Fields, July 2005. View looking north towards Longdale Avenue in the distance. The fields are the site of a new housing development on Swallow Crescent.

Further Reading

Beverley, H. & Jallands, E.   The first fifty years: a brief history of
St. Peter's Church, Ravenshead. 1997.

George, David   The Fishpool Gold Hoard.
Nottingham Topic May 1975.

Jones, Philip E. & Riley, Michael   Newstead Abbey: a portrait in old picture
postcards. 1995.

Lawley, R.S.   Geology of the Ravenshead area.
British Geological Survey. 1993.

Wild, W.   A brief recorded history of Blidworth. 1972.

Ravenshead Newsletter 1970 to present.

Acknowledgments

The compiler wishes to thank the many individuals and organisations who have supplied, and given permission to use, the illustrations in this publication, especially the following:- English Heritage, The British Museum, Nottinghamshire Archives, Nottingham City and Nottinghamshire County Library Services, St. Peter's Church (Ravenshead), Gordon Brown, Ken Buckle, Pauline Burgin, Mary Carter, Mike Chatterton, Bill Flint, Peter Garratt, Marjory Hall, Maureen Kennedy, George Nash, Peter Risdall, Derek Storer, Pat Teager, Ron Walker and John Walton. I would also like to thank Mark Dorrington, Principal Archivist, Nottinghamshire County Council, for his advice and encouragement in this project, and many others without whose help this publication would not have been possible.

Rear cover: Advertisement from the Ravenshead Newsletter, February 1971. Decimalization of currency had been introduced on 15th February 1971.